73

1,000 Black Umbrellas
a collection of poetry

ℭ𝔷

by Daniel McGinn

Write Bloody Publishing
America's Independent Press

Long Beach, CA

WRITEBLOODY.COM

McGinn, Daniel.
1st edition.
ISBN: 978-1-935904-00-7

Interior Layout by Lea C. Deschenes
Cover Designed by Joshua Grieve
Author Photo by Michael McGinn
Proofread by Jennifer Roach and Sarah Kay
Edited by Jamie Garbacik, Courtney Olsen, Alexis Davis, Sarah Kay, and Derrick Brown
Type set in Bergamo from www.theleagueofmoveabletype.com

Special thanks to Lightning Bolt Donor, Weston Renoud

Printed in Tennessee, USA

Write Bloody Publishing
Long Beach, CA
Support Independent Presses
writebloody.com

To contact the author, send an email to writebloody@gmail.com

For Lori

1,000 BLACK UMBRELLAS

1,000 BLACK UMBRELLAS

I

II

I am drawn like blood
into the presence of light.

Press my life like grapes.
Drain me dry.

I

EDUCATION

You don't have to read this.

Reading things you have to read
can make your mind frost up like a windshield
on a cold and cloudy day. You are running late,
the car is warming up and you just want to go.

Reading is difficult because there are too many heavy things to lift.
If a paragraph is both heavy and exciting at the same time,
one can forget to bend the metaphorical legs
and keep the metaphorical back straight,
tiny muscles in the head get strained.

I used to come home from school complaining that my brains hurt.
All I wanted was a hot washcloth and a kiss on my cheek.
My parents used to confront me in the hallway, waving magazines
in front of my face, saying, "If you keep this up,
you will end up wearing glasses for the rest of your life."

Did I listen?
Am I wearing glasses now?

AFTER RAIN
For Paul Suntup

1.
They say
write what you know,
but if you have lived what you know
you don't want to talk about it
to people
that haven't been there.

2.
A good cookie
makes a mess on your shirt.

All of our stories
will crumble like cookies,

leave them laughing
with your crumbs on their lips.

3.
Poetry is quick and
cool as the spaces
between raindrops.

Women will teach you
how to cry
and how to feel better.

You will find yourself
with empty hands
in the desert but for poetry.

4.
Walking to your car
I was watching the gravel
moving below our feet like
an audience.
I was averting my eyes
from a couple embracing,
but they stopped.

I wondered
if we could change history
or even the future.

You sold me a serious book
from the trunk of your car.

5.
When I was young
I was like the bear.

When I was old
I was like the cave.

I carry wind in my mouth.
I form words. I eat the wind.

6.
I remember my father singing
after the divorce:

My love don't give me presents.
I know that she's no peasant.
All she ever has to give
is love forever and forever.
I know she's only fooling.
She's a woman.
She's a woman.

He loved that song.
It made him laugh.

He told me again and again
that women were different than men.
I disagreed.

I was so young.

7.
My father told me
to leave them laughing
and then he bought me a cookie.

LOOSE LIPS SINK SHIPS

Be wrong with yourself
as often as possible,
even when you believe
you are correct.

Line up alphabetically.
Put your short letters first.
Put your long letters last.
Line yourself up in hills.
Line yourself down in valleys.

Stand there silently.
Be seen, not heard,
learn to listen.
We will break your heart.

See how mistaken you are
even when you are truthful?
What do you know anyway?
Not enough—
let that be a lesson to you.

There is your chair.
Go sit in the first row.
I want to see you.

Self Portrait I

I will now paint my fingers
like breadsticks and I will nibble
my serrated nails.

I will sit down here forever; it seems
like an exercise, my legs run in place
and they need something to kick.

Now show me a window
and do not think I will
not jump, because I will.

I will never learn
to paint my colors
inside of the lines
you draw for me.

I have bread in these hands,
my cup runneth all over
the canvas with a splash.

I leap out of the frame,
I am coloring the walls,
I am moving in streaks.

I stand in the corner,
I stand here forever,
paint drops dripping.

MOTHER I

Children open her drawers.
Her drawers are never closed.
Children pull objects from her shelves.
Nothing belongs to her.

Mother drops them to the floor,
children, children, children
always falling at her feet.

She is surrounded.
A blur of fences enclose her,
motion, noise and crying,
children, driven like posts
into the ground.

Children are attached to mouths.
Toothless spittle fresh mouths.
Open mouths want breasts.
These children were born
to warm her
and to be her food.

They want her
to make some memories.
They want her
to give them names.
But she is unraveling,
thread by thread,
pulled this way and that
by the hem of her skirt.
Small hands reach for her blouse
and tear the fabric loose.

PARENTS

I have felt my parents leaning over me
like I'm walking down a narrow street
lined with glass towers.

Have you ever felt this?

I know what it is to die from worry,
to choke down my own thoughts.
I'm not so sure who I was back then,
but I know what I did
must have been wrong.

I feel them watching me.
I keep turning the wrong corner.
It's no wonder I feel lost.
My stomach churns like an ocean
when I see tall buildings
reflected in my glasses.

I think I'd better lie down.
I might drown in my sleep.
The hallways in my lungs
are swimming with fluid.

I dream of you, Mom.
I am floating like a bubble
with an irregular heartbeat.

I dream of you, Pop.
See how much we look alike?
So why are you always leaving?

STAINED GLASS CONFESSIONS

All lined up and all decked out
in the church of incense silence,
meditating on the mystery of my flesh,
numbering the sins under my skin.
Shadows lie draped across the empty pews,
my thoughts are hard and cold as ivory beads
passed between my fingers—

Bless me, Father, for I have sinned…

In the cubed room, dark, quiet as the womb,
robed and seated, the arbitrator listens
calmly propped deep in the chasm
between opposite chambers.
Murmurs float beyond the window curtain.
His son, his brother rises from bent knees.
The light bulb blinks above the door
in the motions of the mystery of forgiveness.

I am a child broken like a sacrament,
many grains of sand melted
smooth as rippled water,
lines of lead fracture my person
like a puzzle that gathers light,
in a church that goes on for centuries.

I feel solar heat warm my shoulders.
I see prisms spill from my chest.
I see Christ crucified.
I see him hanging on the wall to my right.

I remember the ride home.
My slick hair and big ears,
my white shirt and bow tie,
my short legs and shined shoes,
my eyes reflected in the window
against miles of wires and telephone poles.
Tree tops and street signs

repeat themselves in memory
like the smell of incense,
like my small body riding in the back seat,
like the back of my parent's heads.

THE BACK ROOM

Scraped dirt and dry gum dots
from the shopping center sidewalk,
parked my shoeshine stand
beneath a striped barber pole.
It was my business.

Crickets crossed
the concrete, chirping.
The lazy sky was awash
with the hush of sprinklers,
half-lit streetlights leaning forward.

Black dog
slept on the patio
beside the red picnic table,
dreaming of good meals
under opaque wind chimes.

Cricket chirps quickened first,
then came the quiet. There were rats
in the ivy.

Marie would not be able to sleep.
Frank would be getting up at 2 a.m.
coughing up Camel phlegm
leaving in his catering truck.
First a heart attack,
then cancer. His sons were older than me
and liked to beat me up.

I remember crying
in a single bed,
Frank hacking away,
my parents arguing,
drinking, in the Moose Lodge nights.
The smell of Seagram's 7
and accusations.

They were doing this
marriage for the children's sake
if my memories serve me well.

Round back
spinning quarters across blue skies
in chewed up parking lots
where I was supposed to wait in the car.
Dad drank draft,
Lucky Lager,
pool sharking after work.
Quarter closest to the wall won,
took the money home.

Dad had naked women
plastered to the walls
around the desk
in the back room
where I had my first beer:
a 16-ouncer. A tall boy.

Me and the playmates
watched my dad
play poker with his friends,
smiling naked women
peering over my shoulders.

I started parting my hair
closer to the center—
a hustler's part.
I was small for my age.
I used to shine shoes.

MY PART IN THE MUSICAL

My mother liked to dress me. Slacks were required with the school dress code. After school I wanted to wear Levis, just like other boys. Mother was insistent about maintaining a dress code after school. She did not want her son wearing blue collar work clothes. She wanted him to be a doctor or a lawyer. I was in the third grade. I wanted to be an Indian chief, or better yet, a cowboy.

Mother kept a record player on the top shelf of the closet beside a box of records. She loved musicals, especially the ones by Rogers and Hammerstein. My sister and I were weaned on these records and as soon as we could speak we could sing. My father worried about me. Songs like "I Feel Pretty" or "June is Busting out All Over" were fine on a record, but it seemed a bit girlish for a boy to be singing as he danced around the house. He thought, maybe that was why the boys in the neighborhood liked to beat me up. Dad tried to teach me how to box but I wasn't a fighter. I wouldn't play sports. I wasn't coordinated, not at all.

One day three of the neighbor boys were waiting on the lawn when I came around the corner singing, "Doe, a deer, a female deer; ray, a drop of golden sun." My father was watching at the window. He locked the door thinking, this is the only way the boy will ever learn to be a man. The three boys blocked my path. They pushed me and hit me in the back. They kept following me. My father heard me try the door knob. He could hear the boys continuing to push me against the front door. When they began punching me, when my father could hear the thud of fists on flesh, he finally opened the door and said quietly, "That's enough." The neighbor boys ran. I was bent over on the porch crying. My father said nothing. He went to the liquor cabinet and poured himself a drink. Three fingers of Jim Beam, two rocks. My father stood at the kitchen sink drinking and looking into the front yard.

My father did not know that my mother liked to dress us up and take us to the neighbor's houses for impromptu singing sessions. My sister and I were afraid to tell him because our mother would punish us. We were ten months apart, almost twins, which made us cute enough, but when we sang show tunes we were even cuter. Mother decided that her pleasure needed to be shared with the neighborhood bridge ladies. So she dressed my sister in a flapper outfit and a Carol Channing wig. She dressed me in a red, white and blue sport coat, with white slacks and a straw hat. In my mother's eyes, I looked just like Dick Van Dyke in Mary Poppins. The three of us practiced for an hour and then knocked on the neighbors door, interrupting dinner and television time for our quick show. In my mother's mind, this was like having Judy Garland and Mickey Rooney come by for a visit. For the neighbors, it was nothing but strange. My sister and I did not want to sing for the neighbors but we were afraid of our mother. Found ourselves standing in the homes of the neighbors singing a show tune.

I began with, "Daisy, Daisy, give me your answer true. I'm half crazy, all for the love of you. It won't be a stylish marriage; I can't afford a carriage, but you'll look sweet upon the seat of a bicycle built for two. . . ."

My sister, batting her Carol Channing eyelashes, would respond with, "Daniel, Daniel here is my answer true. I'm not crazy all for the love of you...."

It was kind of a creepy show, considering we were brother and sister.

THERE IS NO PEACE FOR WILD THINGS

Inside of me there are no soldiers,
no flags, no governments,
no bombs stealing limbs from children.

We send our offspring
to the other side of the world
and we worry about the price of oil.

We feel pain at the gas pump.
We turn on the television.
We fade away.

There is no peace for wild things.
No field where there was a field.
The frogs are disappearing.

My water smells of chlorine.
Blight has overtaken my garden.

The stars have been replaced
by streetlights and signage.

I was walking the parking lot at a job site
near the Green River in Renton, Washington
when I came across a great blue heron standing
between white stripes on fresh asphalt. He stood
tall as my neck and his eye was prehistoric.
Casting a shadow upon me, he opened his wings
and rose in the air. At that moment I was afraid.

Tonight I set the digital thermostat
and make my bed in America.
I sleep deep and wake to be entertained
by sex, violence, and video screens.

In the global village
the family eats by the television.
There are only crows now.
My childhood creek has grown silent.

Remembering the Taste
of a Blackberry I Ate Last Summer
For my grandfather, whose name I can't remember

I think it took less than a handful of seeds strategically dropped at the side of the creek that roams through the backyard behind my house on Willow Street to create these bramble bushes that arch and dive every which way, weaving leaves and thorns into nature's rebellious unkempt hedges.

It might have been bear shit or it could have been deer shit that brought this gift to my back door, back before there was a back door, or a house, or a road was carved out and paved between the weeping willows. I wish I could have been there.

It's early spring but soon flowers will start to appear. Later I will watch as the flowers disappear. I will ask myself, *Where have all the flowers gone?* It takes a while for a blackberry to mature. God teaches patience to all of us who love blackberries and can't wait to eat them.

A flower hatches a green berry, which becomes a pink berry that turns into a red berry and then the berry turns black: a cluster of niblets, a gathering of fruit bubbles. It's a pretty complicated process.

There was this one blackberry I ate when I was berry picking last summer. My mouth remembers it like it was only yesterday. I picked this berry and balanced it between my upper and lower front teeth. I closed my lips over its bubbles and bit down slowly. The flavors escaped their bubble skins. The first thing that popped into my mouth was the taste of pepper, which was quickly followed by the distinct burst of bazooka gum mingled with barbershop bay rum. I closed my eyes and the smoky tang of cherry tobacco bit me at the back of the tongue—this was the blackberry I had been searching for. Never before had a blackberry rimmed my eyes with Grandpa tears.

My father introduced me to my grandpa, who didn't like to speak if he wasn't getting paid for it. He was a salesman. He had to speak to make a living. If Grandpa wasn't smoking his pipe, he was filling it. Little flecks of tobacco would float from his shirt pocket as he bent down to pick me up. He used to call me Pat or Bill but he seldom remembered my name. That seems fair. I don't remember that much about him.

Grandpa was buried in his favorite suit with bits of cherry tobacco hidden in the lining of his coat and trouser cuffs. If they hadn't buried him in that coffin, we might have had cherry tobacco leaves growing in the hills of California. Grandpa would have liked that.

The funeral was held in an old stained glass Catholic church filled with incense, candles, and Latin prayers. Holy Communion was served to the mourners who were simultaneously sad and serious.

My dad, my mom, and all six kids dressed in black. We opened and closed all of the doors of the family station wagon that served as the pace car for the funeral procession. Everyone started their engines and we followed the coffin up the road to the cemetery. Halfway up the hill, Dad, Mom, and all six kids started laughing like a bunch of manic depressives who had given away their medicine a long time ago. Once we got started laughing, we just couldn't stop.

Here's how the story goes: they took away Grandpa's drivers license. These finger-waggers told him he could no longer drive a motor vehicle. Grandpa bought a golf cart because it ran on a battery instead of a motor and it was sort of street-legal. He drove off in his electric vehicle, rising up the narrow road that ran behind the golf course, figuring he could get to the market by taking the scenic route. Seeing that the sun was shining was occasion enough to start filling his pipe as the golf cart slowly weaved its way up the steep hill. His golf cart veered to the edge of the asphalt and began to tip like the world's smallest SUV. Grandpa rolled down the hill and died in the thorny arms of blackberry bushes.

The generations that followed Grandpa were not afraid to be seen laughing at his life as they drove toward his grave in a funeral procession.

FOOD

Food is important.
Who provides your food?
Where does food come from?
Is it passed through a window
and eaten in your car?
Does anyone care if you are alive?
Who prepared your supper?
Why would anyone feed you?
If you had no money, how would you eat?
Do your cooks speak your language?
Are you nurtured in your native tongue?
Do you crave a glass of milk
when it's time to go to sleep?
How do you sleep?
How about the shape of your heart?
Is it bigger than a breadbox?

HAMBURGER

I'll have mine with a soft drink:
sweet nectar of hard candy,
abrupt with the sighing of bubbles.

Give me potatoes stripped of skin,
damp, eyeless,
cut into dollhouse four-by-fours,
broken up like a home
and tossed into boiling oil.

May I also please
have my meat peeking out the sides,
bulging like love handles?

And a flying saucer made of bread,
that's what I want the top to look like,
like it landed there, a little off-center.

I want ketchup bled on white bread.
I love the way mustard coagulates
with grease and soaks
into the bottom half of the bun.

I like onions chopped into tiny bits,
sharp-edged like shards of glass,
or perfect icebergs poking up
from mayonnaise.

Give me lettuce,
lettuce being to Wimpy
what spinach was to Popeye,
make mine with lettuce

and tomato like a red pumpkin earth,
but I want my tomato sliced
so it looks like a wheel
flopped on its side and brimming with seeds.

Yes, and thank you for asking,
I would like some American cheese on that
because I'm an American
and a hamburger is American food.

The Crows

The crows meet in that tree across the road. They get together
and talk about places to eat. I catch scraps of conversation.
Crows speak of bread crusts and crumbs tossed into the streets,
fruit dropping from the trees, figs exploding on branches.
The joys of searching, green shelter, lizards, beetles, bees,
and the charitable grace of open dumpsters.

Evening crows float from the sky, crows drop quieter than night,
crows fold their feathers up, rest their wings behind their bird hips
and stretch out their twiggy legs.

The butlers of my lawn strut back and forth, back and forth, until
they are only shadows of crows. I haven't figured out why
they disappear at night. They are invisible as the dead,
tucking their heads into a deep black bed of feathers.

Now I Know How a Fish Feels

I've got work to do.
My face faces the window.
Your ghost looks over my shoulder.
The woman across the street
sitting in the dark watching Jeopardy!
learns to answer answers with questions.
She lies like the future lied to the past.
The lies you left behind burn like breadcrumbs
in the bottom of my toaster.
Part of you will always live
in buildings you inhabited.
Flight is a verb that sounds like a bird.
Rain is a noun that falls like a verb
echoing off the triangle pines.
Laughter spills like needles.
Hey, you with the kettledrum throat—
I feel you like a deaf man vibrates.
Hey, you with the metaphor of fish—
we swim in that lake, we sweat like a mirror.
The sky was so dark it hurt my eyes.
Create is a verb; so is destroy.
The world is hushed like a spanked child.
I am alive like a vapor.
My name hangs in the air wherever you spoke it.
Streams split into lifelines.
I look out the window.
I think about gravity and bubbles.

School of Fish

Rainbow scales are sharp
cutting through the flesh.

Dream like fish slip
quick from my grasp.

Hands empty,
aside from the blood,

and the water,
and the humbling.

IN THIS DREAM

I keep catching myself falling,
in this dream I've been dreaming
since my world awoke,

dropped from the womb.
I look back,
and I cry in amazement.

I live in this ship of skin
trapped between two shores.
In this dream I can see

doors of death open
and wave
following wave peak,

like rows of sheep,
like lines of wool,
we are hoisting sail

against the wind.
In this dream
we come and we go.

THE HOLIDAY

Buildings are ghosts.
I live in a building.
I look out the windows I wear on my face.
My eyes dart from left to right like two bees in a jar,
they go *tap, tap, tap,* like fingers on a glass.
I strain my eyes, I close them down like dark apples.

I wear my teal robe backward walking down long hallways.
I drink my pills from a Dixie cup.
I like this place.
This place is clean and structured like a Kubrick film.
The music is classical and the fishing is always good.
I'm so glad we get to talk for an hour on Wednesday.

The faces are turning Fellini out by the apple tree.
It must be spring.
You can open the garage door now.
I think the windshield will be defrosted soon.

ON THE TABLE

I know there was a wind pipe in my throat when I woke up.
I was attached to a machine that was making me breathe
or breathing for me. How do you say it? You can't talk
with that pipe shoved down your throat so I don't suppose
it matters. I counted backward and then they paralyzed me.

Folks wearing masks and colorful caps cut my sternum
open—blue scrubs and gloves leaned in—the music
of pumps was everywhere. I don't know if my ribs creaked
when they cracked me open because I was hardly there.
I doubt that any part of me remembers. I don't know at what point
or for how long the mechanical pump stood in for my heart.
I do know it confuses all of my religious notions about that
muscle. Somehow my aortic valve was removed and discovered
to be bicuspid instead of tricuspid as the Good Lord intended.
This was something I'd suspected for a long time.

Mine was shaped like a communion wafer that would never
fully open and never fully close, yet it kept dispensing blood.
The priest of my body worked faithfully for fifty-five years and then
the priest retired, so if I dreamed at all that day it was fueled
by pure oxygen. My brain had been dying for oxygen for years.
When I started getting dizzy I became afraid the rest of me was dying.
The surgeon took the slack out of the aortic root with Teflon tape.
A tricuspid valve made from pig valve tissue and a plastic ring
was sewed into my silent heart— Saint Jude Medical Model
ESP100-25-00. This miracle happened on my lost day,
January 13th; that number was not in my day planner.
How strange, biggest day of my life and I slept right through it.
Even if they had asked me to watch I'm certain I would have
passed out right away.

POST-OP

I lift with my lower arms,
no more than ten pounds,
reach up for a box of cereal
and the breast bone clicks.

I have grown afraid
of children reaching for my hand.
I am so aware of wires and stitches
I sleep in a reclining chair.
I am afraid of turning on my side.
I am afraid of the sudden
impulses of dogs.
Heart patients get torn in two
vacuuming the rug
or pulling a weed.

I walk for miles;
the legs need to work.
I walk for hours
to keep the lungs clear.
I blow into a tube
and raise the float
ten times per hour.

Thank you for visiting.
I am cautious with hugs.
My lungs hurt without mercy.
My shoulders ache to be used.

DRIVING HOME LATE

The moon keeps following our car
like a mute fish swimming
on a hook and a line.
In the passenger window you glow,
rain-frazzled hair, backlit
by halogen headlamps.

Your hand will not rest tonight
in my hand. The night slips away
speechless. Your hand continuously
shifts positions, tracing my veins,
exploring my fingers, reading my palm,
studying my skin like a book or a wall
in the blind night.

We've been driving for years.
I think to myself. I should tell you
I love you, shy, like the first time.

I keep my eyes fixed on the road.
I know about words;
words would bruise the moment
like a drunk pedestrian
stepping on the flowers.

Anniversary Poem

We watched the sun fall.
We stubbed our toes together.

The earth turned our bodies
the opposite way
bending us backward
until we were doing it,

levitating with feet planted firm like fruit trees
on our blight ravaged drought dry lawn.

You asked for me when leaves were bounding
and blowing from my branches.
We started slowly scraping and slipping down the hill.
The wind kept barking at our heels;

we flapped our fins like seals in heat.
"Will you marry me?" I asked.

She didn't answer with words. She was doing that thing
she does with her whimsical fingers.
She was in her own house then, with her porch lights blazing.
She kept setting the sheets on fire.

Oh man, don't you know? She will always herd my goats.
She puts peaches into my jam.

So where do we go from here? Where do we go for breakfast
after nights like these before her tiny doors close quietly
and one by one, her tiny windows latch?

In Lori's dollhouse heart I started to feel. I turned in my cocoon.
I was hanging upside down but only the sun was sinking,
not me, not my upside down head, not my heart,
not my brand-new touch pad heart.

I am an upright man.
Look at me. Kiss me.
I will open these wings.
I will open them for you.

II

Rainstorm

How do you, the child, process rain?
You, with the memory of water in the womb
so close to the surface of skin.

Wrinkles are the result of water
evaporating from my skin
like the rapture of dots.

Old age is the sound of a thousand men
simultaneously opening black umbrellas.

You, knowing the belly both clothed and naked;
was it less like tears and more like a sprinkling?

Lovers and enemies are rooted in the stomach
like a knee that aches just before the storm.

Can you picture the hand of a man of the cloth
cupping your bald head above the fount?
Now you, the child being carried outside, look up.

Of all the prayers said for me,
did any of them take?
I wish I could believe in you.
I wish I could forgive me.

Someday the one who carries you
will become the one you carry.

Dark clouds splatter in your face.
Don't try to figure it out.
It's not a puzzle or a thing you can chew on;
it's just one more world you're living in.

Turning corners in a stroller,
you lose the sound of your own heartbeat
to the *click, click, click*
of your mother's high heels.

I close the book on another story
that I read to you because it's time for bed.
I talk to myself like I'd talk to a child
and become the father I never had.

INKBLOT

Rub my cheek. I am new:
less mineral, more cloud,
puffed like an éclair.

Saint Augustine stayed green in the summer,
required little attention but made my skin itch—
stick-man arms in pink patch patterns.

I used to climb from the crib
to the top of the dresser
to turn on the radio.

I had a patio, a back porch, a red picnic table, a black dog,
a pink brick fence, a red flower bush, a power mower, and
a big green rake.

I couldn't tell you what was said before *no* meant *no*.
This was before pain had first names.
This was milk on demand, warm skin, and sleep,
plenty of sleep.

Construction paper walls,
the trees outside are bare,
the sand box sand is gray and wet,
I know my colors,
no is *no*.

Here I am in the child's chair.
How many fingers? I have teeth,
I brush them in the morning.
The sink is smaller today.
How many channels?
Kellogg's.
Quick Draw McGraw.
Mine,
these are my toys,
my mom, my lawn, my house—
we don't hit girls.

This is the part where I fall like snow,
my arms have gone to heaven.
You kissed me on the bus;
beyond the windows the world was white.

There were oranges and smudge pots in winter morning.
Stomp my feet between the cracks,
stomp on Lucky Strike pack,
between the trees my breath was fog,
I pretend I am smoking.

Do you remember your fist in my face?
I do.

Your eyes were cold as marbles.
The blood on your shirt was mine.
You were jealous of everything.

My knees were green from Saint Augustine.
Rain fell in my eyes.
Dry leaves and twigs grew out of my hair.

Every finger of mine turned into my fist,
my pulse was beating my fingernails,
my hands were bleeding,
I said what I said, knuckles first,

I kept my heart to myself.

I talked to God, coiled tight as a spring.
Caught in traffic jams of prayers requesting absolution,
an easier ride, or at least a decent parking space.
I talk to God as my engine idles.

I don't know how to play anymore.
My life is confused with
religion and politics.
I hit back until my life was a bruised banana.

Now my father greets me
every morning in the mirror,
his beard turning white as Christmas.

I dress up like my father
and although we seldom talk
we think the same thoughts
and we walk the same walk.

I want clocks to stop and my heart to keep circling.
I look at the sun and moon ticking away
and I remember when.

I don't like what's happened to my body.
I rearrange the furniture behind my face.
The phone keeps ringing but it's never for me.
I keep picking it up.
I keep saying hello.
Almost sixty years and I still don't get it—
where would my thoughts go if I never wrote them down?
Why do people call and say nothing?

THE FAT BOY SINGS

See how circular I become?
Cool as a toad, green as a cucumber,
I lay down a shadow from end to end,
crossing the sidewalk, bending up the buildings.
A shadow implies the presence of sun,
as in Sunday, as in the sun is beating my brow
and bouncing off of asphalt in ripples and waves.

This morning I stepped out the door,
phone in hand, my signal bouncing
off of satellites. This is how my body moves,
how it stops and starts, like red yellow green
every morning here. If I look to my left
I see Disneyland, nine o'clock traffic slowed
by silhouettes in mouse-ear hats.

I call you when the traffic stops moving
hoping to talk to your machine because,
with voicemail, I can say all kinds of crazy shit
without fear of interaction, interruption
or interpretation.

My shadow is an empty cup
leaning over the sink.
My shadow is lying down
in deep pile carpet.
The trick is emerging from my shadow
like fruit and branches.
Keep the legs behind the feet
and keep moving, stop only to shake hands
and say "Excuse me, but I must be going."
Even if I was dying I would need to be on time
and I love you even with all these tears.

I would never have married you
if there was not a little madness in the family.
This is the baggage I carry to our room
where I will always open a door for you.
You know me like you know my shadow,
like my shadow knows you, like we are all
that remains in this world, shadow embracing
shadow after the sun goes down, your branches
tangled in my branches, breathing
and breathing until our breathing stops.

No one is sleeping here except our shadows.
We lie in bed side by side and stare at the ceiling.
You kiss the toad, yet he remains a toad,
after a long hard day.

OUR BED IS A SMALL BIRD SINGING

Your skin is breathing in my hands
so what do I need of metaphors?
Against soft darkness I bury my face
in the peaceful wires of electric night.
The moon is a pearl in your hair.
Light strands descend in streams.
You close the lids of my tired eyes.
I am as welcome as the smell of you.

COMMUNE

Incense pulsing thick
as smoke, we are
as alive as blood,
as sure as a seagull cry,
as long as this mist lingers,
as true as her hands, will always be
outstretched like these tides,
as patient as a circle,
silent as a night settles,
as a mist clings,
as a dark garment is slipped over skin,
over white sand,
winter is wet,
my lover is wet,
dawn is an egg,
cracking open,
winter is waiting
and dripping the light
in her eyes,
as clear
as a full wafer moon.

Pisces Twins

Rejoice that water that flows
    from you, that forms a pool
on the green floor. You on your side
    with spasms of pain pulling,
muscles pulling,

        cold

            drops

    form hot on your flushed face
rolling side to side, the fish,
    the fish are jumping.
    Where is the water, oh where, and
Michael begins the movement

        he dives

            now push.

    Rejoice that child that slides
from our breath and blood to
    swell and grow and Dylan is oh
sliding, oh push the fish on the
    land the fruit of your breasts

        new

           souls.

LIKE THE BEAR

Like the bear
poking his nose around the neighborhood,
this time,
it gets so cold it's freezing all the life
in the still white.

Inside he feels deeply restless,
and outside,
the wind cuts through the fur and sits down
in his bones.
Trees are draped with snow like storage sheets
over raw furniture.

Pressing in close to his cubs sleeping soft
and close
to his mate as the dreams of warm days
slowly fade
into his forehead. He shuts his eyes.

Like the bear,
there comes a time when all becomes
still white.

GRADUATING CEREMONIES: CALIFORNIA HIGH SCHOOL 1995

I need to describe it, how it felt,
sitting on aluminum bleachers,
on the eve of summer solstice.
It was a private thing for the two of us.
I make jokes. I make jokes at funerals.
I make jokes at weddings.

The stadium was filling. I felt surrounded
by voices and footsteps climbing up the stairs.
I was sitting at the aisle with nerve sacks pinched
between my spinal discs.
My body was feeling sore and sad.

My twin sons were wearing blue gowns
and yellow tassels on graduation caps.
They were way across the field.
It was impossible to distinguish them
from the other three hundred students who were
smaller than the names on the program
that I couldn't read without my glasses.

Later, I was holding on to Lori,
leaning on the counter with the coffee brewing.
We cried.
My hand stroked her hair, again and again.
Twenty-one years we had lived together.
Good job, I said.
Dylan stepped into the kitchen;
we straightened up our faces.

My body gave me trouble.
This year I became disabled.
We didn't get them a gift.
We counted our losses and moved into mid-life.

They were going to the beach house.
Soon they will be in Miami, learning
about freedom, staying in a dorm.

Bonnie was leaning on the door to her bedroom.
She has one more year of high school.
She didn't want to come out—
didn't want to be hugged—

these are her brothers,
this is where we live.

A Heart Beating Into Itself

Surgical steel is a thief
cutting the hope
out of the life
on the table.

Hormonal ever after
the doctor removes the womb
and leaves the room
feeling empty.

The heart displaced
silently turns
into itself
like an embryo.

Every instinct whispering,
Nobody's taking
anything
from this house again.

THERE IS NOT A SONG SAD ENOUGH
TO HOLD HER ATTENTION

She smiles at me.

I should know about tears.
I should know about the redness that swallows open eyes.
I should know it like I know my hands know the curve of her.
At night my hands wander up and down the length of her spine.

I should press myself into her sadness.
I should wrap my arms around her.
I should bring her the comfort of skin.
Let this rain fall on me like her hair falls down her shoulders.

I should feel things.
I should know.

To Wake This Short
and Shallow Afternoon

This season of waiting.
My old clock ticking.

Look out the window.
Let the light in slowly.

Write my name,
skate it on glass

with your lithe
frost finger.

The sun creeps low
in the cold sky

causing nymphs
to stir

in the frozen river,
feeding

on silence, they too wait
for gray to turn gold,

for blood to bleed green.
Are we leaves?

Are we grass?
Here a cocoon is frozen

to a twig in a puddle of ice
my foot has cracked.

Somewhere under here
a seed lies dormant.

Will the future bend
my back? Will it be wet?

Will I grow cold?
When winter comes down,

we lift it up.

Skin thin as autumn leaves.
Old hands sprout veins,

struggle with gift wrap and bows.
Please take this thing,

this thing
I got for you.

Tasty Grapes
After Shira Erlichman

Comfort Poem:
Your hair is a silver stream
cutting a passageway
across a midnight pillow.
You dream of coins cascading
down a waterslide into the pool
of your throat. Your breathing fills
the room, sparkling like fish scales.
What a beautiful night.
The curtains gleam like wishes.

Awe Poem:
Touch my beating heart.
Rub the scar.
I am bruised fruit.

Silent Poem:
Suddenly, even the wind
stopped breathing.

Bowl Poem:
soup super rice rose
dust clay beggar's pipe
bong cereal strike spare
toilet

Kite Poem:
String the edges of a crucifix into a diamond.
The skin, paper thin, is folded over taut twine
like a single slice sandwich. Tear your old clothes
into swaddling strips and weigh it down. Keep it
centered. Keep it from spinning. Tie a string to the
center of the cross where the chest would be
if there were a man on the cross, if he had not
risen. Run as fast as you can. Run with all your might.
Slowly release the spool of string. Feel the sky pull

on your hand as the kite grows smaller and smaller.
You look like a bug. Hold on to the string, don't
let it go down. Learn to control it. Teach it to fly.

Always Poem:
We are here
growing old
just like we said we would.

Good Morning Poem:
How many eggs
have we eaten
in all these years
together?

Together Poem:
My breastbone is divided and held
open like butterfly wings with a shiny tool
called a retractor. The surgeon will expose
a bloody beating heart. He does this every day.

This time he will go to work on me. He will crack me
open like a clam and replace my leaky valve and undo
the damage I was born with. My sternum will soon
be closed and stitched back together with stainless
steel laces. These will stay in my chest and be buried
with me. My flesh incision will be closed with clear
sutures that resemble fishing line. Tubes will be placed
in my chest to drain the cavity of normal post-operative
bleeding. I will carry a bag of blood and water like a briefcase
up and down the hospital halls. It will be difficult to breathe.
I will be sent home three days later. A poodle will sleep
on my wound until it is healed. I will talk to the poodle,
a lot, until the poodle is no longer a dog.
The poodle is my nurse and my surprise companion.
The poodle will know this and she will be fulfilled.
She will begin to strut like a small pony and the two of us
will be inseparable, like Mary was, with her little lamb,
the one with the waggity tail.

Love Poem:
Your sleep was warm like a puppy.
Your skin was full of highways.
I drove all night and fell asleep at your wheel.

Whole Poem:
The earth.
The moon.
The stars.
You.

Fart Poem:
It wasn't me.
It must have been the poodle.

Cosmic Poem:
The ocean forms a circle and sings to the island.

Wake Up Poem:
The stream resurrected
is dragged across the pillowcase,
it ripples like water down your perfect back.
Shake your silver hair, it sparkles like coins.
Your feet touch my floor and my floor is blessed.
The sun appears over your shoulder as you sip your coffee.
I watch your lips, like a deer frozen in your headlights,
I watch your lips.

Disappointing Poem:
A car pulls up to the curb.
I look out the window once again.
It isn't you.

Exciting Poem:
You

III

SELF PORTRAIT II

I am crowded in a single bed.
A streetlight peeks through the curtain.

My sibling's steady breathing
is causing the house to creak.

Living with my parents
is like living through an earthquake,

disembodied voices interrupt
our dreams with bickering.

When the house starts shaking
there is nothing I can do

except climb out of my bed
and stand trembling in a doorway

or crawl under a table
and wait for it to stop.

THE BACKWARD SEAT

I never wanted to ride shotgun even when my mother
was the only other person in the vehicle. I didn't like
to sit next to my mother. The third seat in the station wagon
was the backward seat, which was where I liked to sit.
It was the back row in the classroom of the family car.

The front seat had a windshield that pointed to the future.
The third seat had a picture window that faced the passed.
It wasn't enough that I was a weird little kid.
I was also a left-hander in a world that despised
anyone different. My path was blocked by shoe laces,
screw caps and can openers that mocked me.

Most of the things I came across in life
were counter-intuitive, the backward seat
was one of the few places I was comfortable.
It seemed natural to be looking into faces
of people behind their windshields. If anyone
waited at a stoplight they were forced to deal
with me directly. They might pretend not to look
but they were my captive audience.

I might raise an eyebrow, sing like a mime,
or wave like a maniac. Every show was spontaneous.
If the people behind us were in formal attire
I might turn my head and pretend to pick my nose.
If the audience behind us was some poor kid
riding shotgun with his mother I would put my thumbs
in my ears and wave my fingers in the air.

Most of the time there was no one
behind us. I liked riding by myself
in the backward seat. I liked being
alone. When the wheels started rolling
I could watch the past fall behind me,
with my back to the future,
as the front seat was pulling away.

THE PADDLE

Your narrow wooden body
slipped cleanly behind
the couch cushion.

None of us had the strength
to put you there or the will
to pull you out.

We were small
but we stuck together
like mice back then;

when the lights flicked on
we scrambled. We woke
to thunder voices, clinking

glasses, tambourines
in their gospel of hitting.
You were the flag

that waved overhead.
You were the thunk, the thunk,
the thunk, thunk, thunk.

We made a pact to forget about you.
Your disappearance
was a mystery to us.

Even when you were replaced
by the back of her hand.
Even when her ring finger

cut our cheeks.
We maintained the silence.
We never talked.

I Envy Your Thick Morning Cup

How you loved the warm ceramic.
How you held it every morning
like it knew your secret name.

I was a shadow watching as you filled
and drank from it. I was a hollow well.
You took refills around the house
as you shaved and combed
and located your keys.

I envy the barbershop where you slept
in the back room
after you stopped living with us.

You left suddenly.

There was a line of chairs against the wall
where I would wait for you. I remember
your fingers becoming one with thin waist
scissors, the flash of stainless cutting, a comb
forming rows of hair for your fingers to grip
and snip, snip, snip, bright scissor legs, light
shining on stiletto tips, the smooth hand dance
you carried in your wrists.

I have never seen another cup like your cup.
I remember its balloon edges.
I picked it up from the counter and dropped it.
It was nearly weightless.

When you weren't busy cutting hair
you would walk to the pay phone on the wall,
a black heavy steel rotary phone with chrome
coin-shaped circles for nickels, dimes and quarters.
You used to drop a dime, listen for two rings
and hang up. That was your secret code.
You put that dime back in your pocket
and waited for one of us to call you back.

ABUSER

I am the fear inside you.
I am the eye in your keyhole.
I am the face in your window.
I am the click and the deadbolt.
I am the knot you could never untie.
I am the bad dream that followed you.
I am the rock at the bottom of your shoe.
I am the shadow in your mirror at midnight.
I am the gravity that holds your head to the pillow.
I am with you in the photo face-down on your dresser.

These Strangers Behave Like a Family

Everyone looks the other way.
Words squirm behind their teeth.
I feel what they are not saying.
I lift Grandpa onto my shoulders.

Glass bottles and beer cans
lie face up, winking
in the gutter. Here they come,
shiny boot music goose-stepping
behind tanks. Mother starts a
conga line but no one gets
behind her. Father slaps a woman
who turns and punches someone.
I feel the streetlamps burning.

The hills are covered with burnt
sticks and stubble. Nicotine clouds
brush up behind me. "Stop here,
boy," is tongued behind someone's
teeth. "Stop now." I wonder where
the moon went. The sky turns a
darker shade of green. The birds grow
silent. *Lay hands on him. Punch him
again.* I don't obey my thoughts,
I think to myself.

Grandpa lets out a shout
that moves down into my
shoulder blades but I get a
hand up and shove it back
into his soft mouth. His teeth
are hard. When he drops to
the sidewalk the crowd cheers.
I stop. I look. Sometimes I'll
be eating in a restaurant and
I hear his gasp in each sweep
of the fork. When I sleep I feel

his face growing in the wrinkles
around my eyes. In every hand
I shake I feel the bones of his
hands. This is the weight that
rides my shoulders, the child
I carry, everywhere I go.

SELF PORTRAIT III

Look at me, Father,
place my face in your hands.
I do not want to be alone,
I am uncomfortable with strangers.

I have storms inside of me.

My feet are not efficient, Father
and I want to run.
I am not strong or gifted,
I am hobbled like a horse.

Help me.
My hands are hammers,
I crush what I touch.

My head is awash with voices.
I memorize words instinctively.

Here is my darkness, Father.
I have hidden it under a bushel.
Take it.

Take these crumpled bills,
I have fished them from my pocket.
I am a fool with money.

Your mysterious hand
has fallen on my neck
and I cannot lift myself.

The pillow has buried my face
and no one sleeps
at the end of the hall.

Bless me, Father, teach me to cry.
I learned the language of women
but I have not learned to cry like a man.

Allow me to sit quietly
at your passenger side.

I packed myself a suitcase.
I wait where you left me
in a house full of women.

BETWEEN YOU AND ME
for R.M.

You were sitting next to your father
and across from me
when he spoke to me and said,
"That stuff about me in the book?
None of it is true."

It was your battle.
It was all of your life.
He never believed
your part in his life
was true.

I used to see my mother
drink wine, yet she tells
me she never drank,

and she tells me she
has never been drunk
and I never bring up
how she used to yell

and beat me. I never
do because she will
deny it to my father
and she will deny it

to my siblings and
deny it right in front
of my slapped-up face.

I read your book
with great interest
and I didn't even
notice when he said
that.

Not until I saw your face.
I took a picture of your feelings.
I stared at it and empathized
with your eyes. The light
receding.

I do not understand his truth,
I am only concerned with you.
I am sorry.
I am a passive.
Mother would slap me
around from one room
to the next room while
she yelled at me.

I don't tell
nobody,
not to this day.
Not even you.

I never hit back.
I dearly love the women who don't make war.

I look like my father and I laugh
like my father and that woman
he left me with,
she tried to break me
like she broke my father.

My father left her,
and my father left me,
my father left us
for other women.

What was I supposed to expect?
This was supposed to be my puberty.

I will never hit my sisters.
I will never hit my wife.
I love my new family.

You and I are a couple of comedians
with generations of unhappy childhoods
smothered deep inside our blood.

Your father wants to know
how to love you now
but he can't bear the weight
of the stories you bring to the table.

I don't think he can
make himself remember himself
as the man who hurt you.
I think the man he is today
loves you in the clumsy way
that only old men can love.

What kind of fool would turn
from his daughter's face
and give up holding
his daughter's hand forever?
Not me.
No way.

I used to be angry at Mother.
I wanted her to fess up,
to confess, but she never did.
She was never able to see her own shadow.
She refused to believe in my ghost.

So I took her out of that box.
I set her free.
I'll be damned—
I don't know how
to love my own mother.
I never did.

I am not my father.
I am not my mother.
I am none of those people.
I am both of them.

Maybe I should have
gotten in your father's face
and defended your honor.
I am so sorry.
His comment went by unnoticed
until you brought it up.

Everything else was perfect.
I love to see you.
I love to hear you.
My heart is so many kinds of better
when you come around.

Our good friend had just gotten married,
there were flowers on every table,
your father was loving living in your world.
He was digging on your friends,
he was enjoying being in a piece of your life.

What he saw in my eyes
was the only truth I know.
Of course I believe you.
I think he was embarrassed.

There is only so much exposure the human heart can bear,
whether it comes tugging at your sleeve
or just keeps kicking you in the chest.

EVERYTHING OVERLAPS

You fall in love
with someone who knows
the same silence as you,
a silence you share.
They can't see you
so you can't hurt them.

You get sick
of being yourself,
you have to learn
to forgive
yourself first
for whatever the hell
it was you did
that made things
turn out like this.

And you've got to
forgive them too.
It's not so much
anger now,
you can understand
how a person might
grow tired of you.

Maybe you go
to the doctor because
your feet hurt
and you cry so hard
you can hardly
see for days
after you encounter
the person
who abandoned you.

A letter arrives
addressed to you
with layers
of frustrated tape
pressed to the seal.

Maybe you are just a dog
after your own tail.
Maybe you thought
you were done looking back
at shadows;

they come to your door
like snow clouds.
You open the door,
it's cold outside,
but you stand there
waiting to see
what is going
to happen,

because you've
lived in this town
all of your life
it's never snowed here,
not once.

YOU, READING A GOOD BOOK
WITH RECORDS ON THE FLOOR

You haven't attended the church of your choice
in so many years that everyone has stopped
asking about you. You don't visit your parents
anymore. They never visited you.

You stay home and read a good book. You like
old records but you seldom put them back
in their sleeves, let alone the slip jackets. It's
too much work. This is your time off.

You like to listen to slow ballads about how you
laid around and played around this old town too
long. You like pops and scratches. The last time
you saw your mother, her face was so old she kept
repeating herself.

How old are you? you ask her. *76 Trombones!*
she replies. *76 Trombones!!* she replies again.
It keeps coming back to you in idle moments
during lunches eaten in such silence
even radio doesn't help.

You will always remember that remark. The way
it slid from the wrinkled corner of her mouth, her
light blue watery eyes. She has twenty-five trombones on
you. That sing-song moment will follow you
to your grave.

A TRUE STORY

I'm 55 and my father is 83.
I just had heart surgery nine days ago.
My dad is over for a visit with Leigh,
the woman he lives with.
I have to walk at least sixty minutes a day
and I can't sit any longer.
I have to move.

Leigh tells Dad, who just opened a beer,
that he should go too, and he does.
He steps out into our suburban neighborhood,
beer in hand, wondering where we are going.
At the end of the block he sees the liquor store
across a six-lane highway
and he wants to run across the street
to get a lottery ticket. He buys one every week.
I don't want to run across the highway or wait
while he does so I point out another liquor store
just around the corner. We go there.
I wish I was carrying money
because I would like to buy a ticket too.
I haven't really bought a thing
or gone anywhere since the surgery.

As we approach the entrance
Dad hands me his beer
and tells me to sit on the electrical box
and wait for him.
I was 12 and my Dad was 30.
The beer was really a Pepsi
and the liquor store was really a bar.

MOTHER II

She was my first meal and my best guide.
Nobody loved me like Mother did.
I could tell her about everything
that went wrong. I could finally get it out
but she would not remember now.

She would forget what she just said to me
and she would say it again, even if I told her it hurts.
She would say the same thing again and again.

This is the train where the brakeman died.
We've been rolling downhill at least ten years now.
She was much younger then, she could still fetch a man.
She could tell when her food had begun to mold.
She hates to throw out food.

She tosses her scraps on the lawn for the dog to eat.
The dog has been dead for years.
She keeps trying to remember that dog's name.
She has forgotten the names of people in pictures on her wall.

She wants to light you a fire.
She wants to drive you in her car.
She wants to help you cook her dinner.

You are the child who will always let her.

She puts the bones back in your soup.
She turns off the oven as soon as you turn your back.
She takes your pie and offers you a slice,
she tells you it was a gift from somebody else.

You bite your lip,
you don't disagree,
you wonder what will happen to your mind.

IV

AMATEUR SURREALIST I

The earth around the feet of the bus bench is turning round,
soft, pink and Texas-grapefruit-round,
where the amateur surrealist sits under the tulip moon
waiting for some inspiration to arrive.
He cannot afford a car.

A bird leg disguises itself as a tree,
hides behind the bench, its bumpity trunk stands erect,
hollow bones overshadowed by feathery leaves
that chirp and coo and gather together
like thousands of shoppers that drift and twirl
in a descending downward curl.
They stick to the mulky pulp like bad betting slips.

Meanwhile, a happy claw grip
is hammering down roots
into the mushy prey of a dying grapefruit. It stinks.
The amateur surrealist notices the smell, feels fowl wind
breathing up and down his neck, his throat is scratching
like a chicken, he keeps checking his watch for ants,
his face is not melting. He looks up and down the street.
His persistent tongue is hanging out of his shoes, his feet
indignant now, and thirsty, his laces passionately unraveling,
coupling and uncoupling, twitching like cheap rubbery worms.
He writes these words and they taste like chicken.

The earth is not a fish, and birds are not so easily fooled.

It rhymes.

Leafy Moments (A Bakers Dozen)

I
I bought a tree online.
It arrived the next morning
fully equipped with leaves.

II
One week later
I received an e-mail
from one of the leaves
asking for more water.

III
This leaf
became a spokesleaf
for the others.

IV
The sun shines
through the window.

The leaf is green.
Light is warmth.
Alive is good.

V
The leaf is on the tree.
The tree is on the table.
Kermit is on the TV
strumming on the old banjo.

VI
My parakeet
cocks its head
and ponders the leaf.

The leaf
is shaped
like a feather.

VII
Take the tree outside.
Here comes the wind.
The leaf gets all excited
and starts wagging its tail.

VIII
Soil and roots are one.
Tree and leaf are one.
Sun and milk are one.
Breakfast for everybody!

IX
Evening shadows fall on the leaf.

X
A blackbird sleeps
on the windowsill;

in the blink of an eye
it opens its wings.

XI
The green leaf stands up
like an arrowhead.
All of its fountains
have turned into gold.

XII
Frost and window are one.
Stem and branch were one.
Leaf and air are one.

XIII
The leaf has leapt.
The room is full of circles.

Amateur Surrealist II

The amateur surrealist gritted his teeth, gritted his teeth
until his teeth were spider webs
as he pushed a small cry
away from himself. It was not his cry,
he pushed it back out of his inner ear.
With a pop into the pink it skittered off like a seahorse
in a bubble and spray of sky.
It was a small

cry

but a cry with a mouth of its own,

blushing across the cheek like the tingle that follows
the slap. Close the lids of your eyes
and you will see in the dark chocolate
how the mind draws everything back
into the ears. Sounds spin
like cotton candy, voices swim
like sperm
in the ear canal where thought breaks down
into waves.

This is the tunnel
where the amateur surrealist was hard at work
pushing a sound with tiny hands
out of his inner ear, loosing a cry
suddenly unleashed like a gold cross
suddenly unclasped from its chain,
arms extended, eternal 3:15, the sky
turning away, turning away like an analog clock,
a diver rising up from the pool,
the earth reaching up, slapping his face,
filling his fists, with dust.

GOD SAVE THE QUEEN

I feel sorry for the leaves
that sailed from your tree into my backyard.
Sorry for the beautiful colors scraping messages on my windows.
Sorry for the cruel wind that blows them back into your yard.
Sorry that I did not take a rake and scoop their crisp dead bodies
into a garbage body bag.

That's what I told the landlord
when he knocked upon my door
with his mustached eyeball
and his ring full of keys.

Sorry, I said to his eyeball.
I apologized to his shadow
ringed in autumn light
when he pushed his halo face
against the crack in my door.

I apologize for shaking the jar
and for the small fires that stopped and started.
I apologize for scrambling the ants
and making them war with each other.

They communicate, you know.
I could hear them running amok
and screaming bloody murder
as I stood there at the kitchen sink.

I watched the ladle
swirl the sugar
into a jug of Kool-Aid.
That was my dinner.
That's what the ants wanted.

I apologize for being raised indoors
and buying food in hermetically sealed containers.
I apologize for being weak of heart and stomach.
I apologize for running away and allowing my dog
to continue without intervention.
I think that is proof that I was totally unprepared
and as surprised by Snuffy's actions as you were.

I never talked to the dog about you.
Snuffy is not a puppet;
I wasn't controlling the dog.
We just want to be free.

I apologize for Snuffy who wants to be free.
I am so sorry I took off the leash
the day she bagged a small fawn
and dragged parts of it on to your front porch
tearing off tufts of fur and spreading them
across your perfectly manicured lawn.
I am sorry about the smears of blood and meat
that left brown stains on your doorposts.
I apologize for the carcass in your driveway
and the nest of flies it drew.

I must also apologize for the ants
that march around in my brain.
They are following directions from the mysterious one.
They communicate with each other but not with me.
They have their marching orders.
They are focused on the queen,
may God save her.

AMATEUR SURREALIST III

They come back again
painting the crimson town
with violets and clouds, filling the sonic sky
with their scarlet
booming
voices.

The amateur surrealist is up in arms
standing at the crossroads. He shouts demands
at all of them, shaking his fist, his starved wrist bones pop,
his fingernails laugh at him, rattle like tambourines,
his hands shake the snakes from the ivory wind,
his eyes crack open like egg shells, yolk dripping down
filling the dark pores inside his eyes, his face burning
from stars washed down his face every night,
washed down with wine under the bridge every night,

every night so chilly for the amateur surrealist,
even the wind whistling through his teeth burns.

Stand Me Up

My eyelids open.
I jabber to myself like a man of prayer.
My punctuation is broken.
My syllables snap like sticks.
My words pile up like stones.

Touch fingertips to fingertips,
make a steeple.
My prayers are invisible like God.
My prayers are conceptual like church.
My prayers ascend like crows.
My prayers fly through the air like fists.

My prayers shake free
and run around the room like a hyperactive child.
My prayers cannot sit still.
My prayers cannot be taught.
My prayers are small.
My prayers are silent as milk.

My prayers flare up on a match head.
My prayers rise like smoke
from a cigarette I hid in the toy box
beneath discarded limbs
and hollow torsos of dolls.

My eyelids rock on smooth hinges.
Prayers fill my eyes like lost balloons.
My eyebrows are black and hard as brushes.
Tip me back and lay me down,
my eyelids slide shut,
I squirt tears from glassy eyes.

I simulate sleep.
My prayers fall to the floor like a clumsy glass of wine.
My head is crawling with dreams that sprout and curl
like nylon tufts from the dark holes in my detachable head.
My prayers stain the carpet red.

My prayers follow me around like a bread crumb trail.
My prayers end abruptly.
My prayers are swallowed by birds.

AMATEUR SURREALIST IV

There is a woman in the window where the glass is always warm.
The amateur surrealist, he comes to her again,
he comes to her for clarity,
he comes and he comes unattached
from himself. A translucent Harpo,
mirroring the faint smile, mimicking his hesitant
steps, the baggy pants, the lumpy coat,
the upturned collar, the bee clinging stubbornly
to the black of his sleeve.

And her, so cold, so aloof, calm, frozen, balanced
between the ball of her right
step and the turn of her left
toe, detached as a bird's egg, fragile
as a small planet, so complex and beautiful. Her skin
so smooth, the tilt of her head, her face like an angel.
The amateur surrealist is held sweetly in time
surrounded by banquet table blues overflowing
with white carnations.

This is how it feels. This is how it feels.
He touches and he touches, brings his hand to the table,
warm and smooth as glass, again he comes to her.
She hardly notices the amateur surrealist watching over her.
And the woman in the window is not moved.

It Starts Like This

No, she says, *it's not you, it's me.*
I say, *What do you want from me?*
She says, *In God there is no shame*
and there is no shame in loving a god.
So I want to be like God,
god-like, speaking life into being.
I am trying to hide myself between words.
She is trying to inch her body between rain drops.

It's raining too hard for that now.
It's raining about the bodies.
It's raining animal instinct.
It's raining so hard it makes her damp.
It's raining so hard she can't see me.
She's looking me right in the eyes.
She's got somebody else.
She's got somebody else pressed against her body.
She's talking to a stranger
saying that he could be somebody else.
He's anybody else but me.
I watch as she rubs her question against him.

You see,
I want to be like God, god-like.
God is never surprised,
God is forgive forever;
being a man is hard.

I know what it is to be anybody else.
I'm no saint with my mind floating away from my body,
floating above anybody else lying spread eagle below me.
She wants death without dying,
much more intense than love,
much more mouth, much more electric,
mouth, mouths,
more,
electric.

There is a *God, oh God,*

                     oh God,

you feel so good.

This is what anybody wants.
This is what the forsaken fear.
Today I am the dead man who wishes he didn't know
about how blood rushes to her nipples
when they are swollen pink,
unbelievably pink.
I kissed them and they were holy,
I held them behind my teeth
like a secret that grew on my silenced tongue.
I remember her small hand rising straight up my back
and dropping in the arc of a wave.
I held her like the question I was born to answer
again and again.

I am the dead man.
I am in love with her.
I wish I was a god.
I wish I was good.
Oh my God,
I wish I was a stranger.

AMATEUR SURREALIST V

Dissatisfied, under the black light,
the amateur surrealist shuffles silently to the confessional.
It is dark and his molars glow. He's got his back up now.
His molars grow. He looses his tongue like a tortured finger,
pointing it at his poor nameless mother, still bottle-feeding
the back of his mind. The interior of his mouth is milky, drab
and sparsely furnished. This is no place to live.
His thorny tonsils hang sharply like mistletoe,
all cubist angles and absurd. There is a priest in this picture.
There is the back of his head. He does not communicate.
He is wrestling, restless with words, unable to speak anything
but meaning, he is a nice man, unable to define anybody's sin,
knowing nothing but his own, he speaks not a word
but in sentences. He rattles his cup on the bars.
He cries for water
for forty days and forty nights.
No tears come. No one is holding him.

For the amateur surrealist, this is the dry season.

SELF PORTRAIT IV

The slow velocity
of a gleaming knife,
flipped in the hand
and pressed to flesh,
like a doorknob.

What is with the other hand
coupled to a fork
that will pierce, pick
and prick the food on my table
hundreds and hundreds of times?

What is the story
locked in the hunger
that climbed out of my cradle
pajamaed in gibberish
with longings awash
in the river's innocence?

Here is my breath,
baptismal wet,
my toothless drippings
slipped under the chin.

I wake the kid up,
we do some dancing,
we put down the knife,
we crayon some Picasso.

Everyone is sleeping.
We are not afraid to cry.

Amateur Surrealist VI

The inconspicuous ink
stain crept quietly unnoticed from the wrong side of his shirt pocket.
There was a shadow on a street where the sun shone smartly,
worthless and shiny like a bright copper penny
dropping down a hole in the trouser pocket
into the dark night of the sole of the amateur surrealist's shoe,
the sole that separated the surrealist from the shadow on the earth,
the shadow that began to leak like a dark cloud,
turning into a hand, turning into a rabbit from the hat,
turning a lily into a fist.

The amateur surrealist can feel the shadow watching,
listening to his every last word, like a policeman,
like a therapist; the shadow sees every crack
in the sidewalk, the shadow sees the sun burning
a hole in his shoe, the shadow spreads like an ink stain,
the shadow hovers over him like a net ascending,
the shadow is jam packed with dark fish flapping,
the shadow is full of fins and pin-prick teeth and smiling
night dreams and mouths full of scales and blood.

The shadow spills across the sidewalk, fish
skipping over hopscotch chalk, the shadow multiplies
into enough screams to fill a multitude.
The shadow sees every sparrow that hits the dirt
and all the hairs and all the lice of his days
are numbered like wrists, like badges,
like smoke, like flames.

DREAMING OF WARSAW

Night breaks down into a murder of crows.
You talk in your sleep with a Polish accent.
Dark fruit drops from the shadow trees.
You ask me for tea with two lumps please.

You talk in your sleep with a Polish accent.
You fidget in sleep with each siren's pass.
You ask me for tea with two lumps please.
Your breathing is marching like boots in a village.

You fidget in sleep with each siren's pass.
Dreams lie in shreds, claws on black paper.
Your breathing is marching like boots in a village.
Black dogs held back by black leather leashes.

Dreams lie in shreds, claws on black paper,
multiply stench by the shaking of trains.
Black dogs held back by black leather leashes
walk the banks of the hungry human river.

Multiply stench by the shaking of trains.
Explode the hinges and my dream slaps the floor.
Walk the banks of the hungry human river.
Naked in my kitchen as they search for the children.

Explode the hinges and my dream slaps the floor.
Dark fruit drops from the shadow trees,
naked in my kitchen as they search for the children,
my night breaks down into a murder of crows.

V

I Will Come

I will come from you
but you will not know
where I came from.

I will dance
in the sweetness
of your native tongue.

You will speak another language
with the birds of your hands.

You will swim another ocean
with the wings of your feet.

I will come to you
when you step outside
into the breathing world
where it just rained.

I will circle you with wind.
I will hold you in the air.

Let your brow unfurrow
over bright morning eyes.
Your green will rise up
sprouting from the dirt.

You will be released.
You will be relieved.
You will be happy.
Your burden will be lifted.

Let it come out now.
Watch it fly from your hands.

WHITE CROW FEATHER

The page is blank.
Everything she writes is white as walls.
The lily in the white vase is alive.
The well is an inkwell filled with milk.
Her cursive is correct.
She dips the quill.
She writes an ode to silence
on a white piece of paper.
As she writes, the words disappear.
She mouths the words
until her mind is blank.

MERCURY MOUTH

There is an ocean
where her voice had been.

See the empty bottles
strewn along the shore.

I listen for messages
the water washed away.

I sit there for hours
waiting for the next wave.

White seagulls pepper themselves
into a flock of pigeons.

That's how we are, you and I,
surrounded by stains and sand.

The nurse arrives, dressed like the moon
in her white smock.

I open my arms.
She keeps bleeding me.

My tributaries empty
into her presence.

SELF PORTRAIT V

I carry these paperbacks
like I carry you
just in case
I find a moment free.
I've had my nose in someone's book
ever since I could read.

I am in the library
when my phone begins to vibrate.
I would pick it up but I know it isn't you.
You know where you might find me,
at a table for one.

Television chatter always makes me lonely.
My metabolism keeps changing my feelings for you.
The days grow short, the naps grow longer,
my alarm clock just sits there not saying a word.

I wake up like a ghost town, my windows choked in dust.
You live in a village that I will never visit.
I would raise my voice but it wants to say your name.

We sit side by side on two different trains.
You are always there and I always never catch you.
The sun rises in the dark,
the moon lingers in the daytime,
it is never the right time
to feel the way I do.

Loneliness Between Poems

There are weeks when every word is nothing but a shy child,
a small eye peering from behind, around the pleated cloth.

There are weeks when words don't even approach me;
we pass on the street mute, like old lovers.

I have spent too much time with words sitting across the table,
words too polite to reach for, words too timid to ask.

I pace in and out of all the rooms in my apartment wondering what,
and when, and which words will come.

I hurry across the street before I notice the sign says "Don't Walk."
I think that there has to be a nature poem somewhere in this heart of mine,

words with long boots, words with warm socks,
words with days where we walk together.

Rain All Week

A part of me is not awake,
a part of me is dreaming, the rain
is making an awful lot of noise,
a suicide leap lasting for days.
Days fall and collect into rainbow
pools on black asphalt, potholes
under water, tire wings crossing
the lake, off I go, I step, I accelerate,
I brake, all around me, the skid,
the slide, the thump
of steel and plastic.

There is a lake beside the house
where we wade to the water heater
and relight the flame. We listen
for gas to ignite, for fingers of fire
to keep the captured water warm.
My car heater is slow to react,
clouds climb into my car, cling
to the windshield like a swarm
of insects that are dying to get out.

I cannot see, I have things to do,
part of me is still in bed, still under
covers, part of me wakes up to listen
to my bones creak like a rocking chair,
to listen to tiny hammers pounding
in my ears, tapping on my windows,
pebbles by the fistful come
tumbling down my roof.

WHEN THE CHILD SANG

When the child sang, she made darkness come.
The melody was different than anything heard before.
Her voice unearthed the pain in people.
Ancient hurts were resurrected.

If a flute could learn to groan like a cello,
it would still not be as odd and unnerving
as the graveness in her little voice.

The toddler sat up and leaned her weight
back on the bars of her crib.
With a blank stare she slowly started
to release the song that was trapped inside her.

She held its rhythm in every breath.
The music was a river flowing in and out of her essence.
She never moved to the music.
She was lost in her work.

She did not know what her plump hands were doing.
Fingernails dug deep into her palms.
Fingers would open and gesture from time to time.
Fingers would bend out in unison like she was holding out a gift.
Her palms would press against her chin.

This was not dramatic,
the singer was more like a typist. She never looked.
Her eyelids fluttered and her pupils hid behind them.

Her song turned white and cold like the belly of a trout.
She sang of the hook digging.
She sang of a trickle of blood staining the water.

The fish in the aquarium stopped looking for food.
They lined up at the glass and waited.
Then the light bulb in the fish tank died.

Maybe someone should have stopped her.
Her parents were out.
The babysitter was terrified.

Imagine hearing a toddler sing a dirge from a crib,
a song that caused flowers to wilt their petals and cover their seeds.
Crickets on the patio silenced themselves
and rotated their heads as one
out of a fear of that sound.

When the porch swing swayed slowly the house whispered too.
Secrets were out on the wind and every soul that had passed
through the doors of that home where the child sat singing
began to hear her desolate cry.

Not with the ears, it was more like what a deaf mute hears
when someone they love enters the room.
The child's song, like all our songs, was nothing more than vibrations.
That's all it was and it did not last for long.

The child never wondered why mother was anxious
or why father always wanted to cry but never did.

She was too young to understand such things.
She was too young to express her own sorrow,
she had yet to really live and she had yet to really die.

WIND AND THE WINDOW

I cannot tell you why
my throat started humming
like a bird on a neon sign.
Hollowness slipped off of my shelf
with the silverware.

You were far away.
You were talking.
The wind moved on my neck,
I remembered your hands.
I cannot tell you why dust
settled on the furniture.

Hollowness shook us
like an earthquake.
I looked across the room
and you were laughing.
Your face
was in the window
opening.

I cannot tell you
why every noise startled me
but hollowness lifted
 us like a wave.
You were next to me.
You were talking.

The wind
in the window
opened.

I Tell You I Love You

You don't want to hear it,
not now,

you tell me this vocation is growing us old,
leaving us alone, without love, without money.

You tell me life is without love, writing a poem
is firing a shotgun and swallowing both barrels.

Brautigan, his spirit broken, closed the door
and did it in the back room.

Plath fell asleep in her kitchen
resting her head in a cold oven.

Our chests are made for ripping,
our insides are a fire,

what we do is not to be loved,
what we do is not for money,

I tell you I love you,
I ask you to go on living.

THE NAME THAT MAKES US CRY

I predict
that someday we will all lose somebody
and we won't know where to find them.

This will be the shadow that will follow us
everywhere we turn.

I predict
that we will be surprised
that the clothing in the closet is free of flesh.

Our days will be as strange as the silence of the cane
hooked to the handrail at the foot of the stairs.

AS LONG AS I LIVE

I will never be comfortable
with the way you looked
at me, your swollen eyes
peering out of a hospital bed,
white walls, white sheets,
the bright blue blanket tucked
tight, everything awkwardly
out of place.

I sat stiffly in an uncomfortable
chair with my back to the long
window that looked out over
the parking lot. There was no
indication of peace in your eyes
as you told me of your decision
to shut down the machine that was
breathing for you.

Your anger
was as visible
as the lack of tears
this time.

Life is not fair, you said
to your mother, standing
in the open door, your black
hair spun into Mary Pickford
ringlets that bobbed with each
sad desperate breath you took,
as tears shook free from
your childish eyes.

THE CHAIR

The empty chair reflected
in the television screen
is growing old.
Its foot rest is broken
and it misses your mother,
her flannel nightgown,
her oxygen hose
snaking across the arm,
 no longer resting
on the cushion.
This chair, this reminder
you almost threw away,
is always occupied.
The chair that can't stop breathing
misses your mother.
The chair is inhabited
by a sleeping poodle
when everyone is gone away
until the great-grandchildren
pool together and squeeze
into her lap,
with their pajamas and their cereal,
with their juice box and saltines,
their cartoon eyes oversized
by feel-good talking animals
that flicker across the screen.

They relinquish the chair
when I walk in the room
just like they have always
seen you do.
They move to the couch
and I fall asleep
to the slow pace
of Little Bear and Dora,
the poodle too,

we both fall asleep in the chair.
I eat dinner in the chair
and when the poodle and I
retire to the bedroom
you sit in the chair
in your flannel nightgown.
When ice cubes float
in your two-dollar wine
the chair is just fine.

BLOOD RIVER

After I died I dwelled in all of my dwellings
from all of my lives all at the same time,
when I turned my head I would be standing,
or crawling, or sitting in a different room,
my room that kept changing, all the time.

If I were to blink, my walls would become
windows into all of my streets, all of my yards,
where all of my mothers, and all of my fathers,
and all of my children could congregate.

See the leaves rise up from the ground
and retake their places in the arms of bare trees,
smell the moisture in the air, everything that was
rained upon is steaming with sunshine
and everything smells so clean.

I close my eyes and watch light streaming down
between the branches of redwood trees. I know
what these trees are saying like I know my own name.

I reach to touch your hand, your face, but you are
sitting by the side of my hospital bed. I wish I could
give you my physical heart, the one I was born with.

At first I hid my heart in a house I made of Lincoln logs;
later I hid it in cupboard in a house where we made love,
and babies, and arguments, but soon the house fell down
and the pieces were taken to the city dump. I almost died.

I placed my physical heart into the hands of all the people
I ever became but they fought with each other because
they all thought they owned my heart. The doctor had to
cut me open to repair my heart. Now I see, I never owned
any part of my body—it always belonged to you.

I have reached the end of my shelf life but I still taste
the blood beginning to flow through my arms and legs.
I no longer hear the blood river leaping over dams.

My spirit can clear the dams.
You and I are liquid glass.
We are always falling, we will go on,
we will never break.

ACKNOWLEDGMENTS

"After Rain" appeared on *The Big Damn Poetry Slam CD*.

"There Is No Peace for Wild Things"was published in *The November 3rd Club* (november3rdclub.com).

"School of Fish" was published in *Talus and Scree*.

"On the Table" was published in *Sage Trails* and *Don't Blame the Ugly Mug (the Two Idiots Peddling Poetry Anthology)*.

"Driving Home Late"was published in *Blue Satellite*.

"Rainstorm" and "The Fat Boy Sings" were published in *Tide Pools, A Collection of Orange County Poetry*.

"Pices Twins," "Like the Bear," "Graduating Ceremonies" and "A Heart Beating Into Itself" were all published in *Ester*.

"Tasty Grapes" was "The Friday Love Poem" in the online blog *The Serotonin Factory* (theserotoninfactory.blogspot.com).

"The Amateur Surrealist" appeared in *Spillway* and *Talus and Scree*.

"Dreaming of Warsaw" appeared online at *The Poetry Super Highway* (poetrysuperhighway.com/PoetLinks.html).

The author would like to thank Bonnie Saunders and Rachel McKibbens for their invaluable proof-reads and editing suggestions. Thank you for making it happen.

The author would also like to thank The House of Designers (HouseofDesigners.com) for creating his website.

Visit my website: themcginnshow.com

About the Author

DANIEL MCGINN is an old school poet based in Orange County, CA. His work has appeared in numerous journals and anthologies including *So Luminous the Wildflowers* and *Beyond the Valley of the Contemporary Poets*. He was a journalist for the *East Whittier Review*, the *OC Weekly* and *Next Magazine*. He has hosted poetry shows across Southern California and performed at a variety of venues such as The Bowery Poetry Club in NYC and The Fuse in Philadelphia. He has had five chapbooks included in the Laguna Poets Series. *1,000 Black Umbrellas* is his first full length book of poetry. Daniel is a maintenance coordinator at a paper recycling plant; he is also a poet.

New Write Bloody Books for 2011

Dear Future Boyfriend
Cristin O'Keefe Aptowicz's debut collection of poetry tackles
love and heartbreak with no-nonsense honesty and wit.

38 Bar Blues
C. R. Avery's second book, loaded with bar-stool musicality and brass-knuckle poetry.

Workin' Mime to Five
Dick Richard is a fired cruise ship pantomimist. You too can learn
his secret, creative pantomime moves. Humor by Derrick Brown.

Reasons to Leave the Slaughter
Ben Clark's book of poetry revels in youthful discovery from the heartland
and the balance between beauty and brutality.

Birthday Girl with Possum
Brendan Constantine's second book of poetry examines the invisible lines
between wonder & disappointment, ecstasy & crime, savagery & innocence.

Yesterday Won't Goodbye
Boston gutter punk Brian Ellis releases his second book of poetry,
filled with unbridled energy and vitality.

Write About an Empty Birdcage
Debut collection of poetry from Elaina M. Ellis that flirts with loss,
reveres appetite, and unzips identity.

These Are the Breaks
Essays from one of hip-hops deftest public intellectuals, Idris Goodwin

Bring Down the Chandeliers
Tara Hardy, a working-class queer survivor of incest, turns sex,
trauma and forgiveness inside out in this collection of new poems.

1,000 Black Umbrellas
The first internationally released collection of poetry
by old school author Daniel McGinn.

The Feather Room
Anis Mojgani's second collection of poetry explores storytelling and
poetic form while traveling farther down the path of magic realism.

Love in a Time of Robot Apocalypse
Latino-American poet David Perez releases his first book
of incisive, arresting, and end-of-the-world-as-we-know-it poetry.

The New Clean
Jon Sands' poetry redefines what it means to laugh, cry, mop it up and start again.

Sunset at the Temple of Olives
Paul Suntup's unforgettable voice merges subversive surrealism
and vivid grief in this debut collection of poetry.

Gentleman Practice
Righteous Babe Records artist and 3-time International Poetry Champ
Buddy Wakefield spins a nonfiction tale of a relay race to the light.

How to Seduce a White Boy in Ten Easy Steps
Debut collection for feminist, biracial poet Laura Yes Yes
dazzles with its explorations into the politics and metaphysics of identity.

Hot Teen Slut
Cristin O'Keefe Aptowicz's second book recounts stories of
a virgin poet who spent a year writing for the porn business.

Working Class Represent
A young poet humorously balances an office job with the life
of a touring performance poet in Cristin O'Keefe Aptowicz's third book of poetry

Oh, Terrible Youth
Cristin O'Keefe Aptowicz's plump collection commiserates and celebrates
all the wonder, terror, banality and comedy that is the long journey to adulthood.

OTHER WRITE BLOODY BOOKS (2003 - 2010)

Great Balls of Flowers (2009)
Steve Abee's poetry is accessible, insightful, hilarious, compelling,
upsetting, and inspiring. TNB Book of the Year.

Everything Is Everything (2010)
The latest collection from poet Cristin O'Keefe Aptowicz,
filled with crack squirrels, fat presidents, and el Chupacabra.

Catacomb Confetti (2010)
Inspired by nameless Parisian skulls in the catacombs of France,
Catacomb Confetti assures Joshua Boyd's poetic immortality.

Born in the Year of the Butterfly Knife (2004)
The Derrick Brown poetry collection that birthed Write Bloody Publishing.
Sincere, twisted, and violently romantic.

I Love You Is Back (2006)
A poetry collection by Derrick Brown.
"One moment tender, funny, or romantic, the next, visceral, ironic,
and revelatory—Here is the full chaos of life." (Janet Fitch, *White Oleander*)

Scandalabra (2009)
Former paratrooper Derrick Brown releases a stunning collection of poems written
at sea and in Nashville, TN. About.com's book of the year for poetry

Don't Smell the Floss (2009)
Award-winning writer Matty Byloos' first book of bizarre, absurd, and deliciously
perverse short stories puts your drunk uncle to shame.

The Bones Below (2010)
National Slam Champion Sierra DeMulder performs and teaches
with the release of her first book of hard-hitting, haunting poetry.

The Constant Velocity of Trains (2008)
The brain's left and right hemispheres collide in Lea Deschenes' Pushcart-Nominated
book of poetry about physics, relationships, and life's balancing acts.

Heavy Lead Birdsong (2008)
Award-winning academic poet Ryler Dustin releases his most
definitive collection of surreal love poetry.

Uncontrolled Experiments in Freedom (2008)
Boston underground art scene fixture Brian Ellis
becomes one of America's foremost narrative poetry performers.

Ceremony for the Choking Ghost (2010)
Slam legend Karen Finneyfrock's second book of poems ventures
into the humor and madness that surrounds familial loss.

Pole Dancing to Gospel Hymns (2008)
Andrea Gibson, a queer, award-winning poet who tours with Ani DiFranco,
releases a book of haunting, bold, nothing-but-the-truth ma'am poetry.

City of Insomnia (2008)
Victor D. Infante's noir-like exploration of unsentimental truth and poetic exorcism.

The Last Time as We Are (2009)
A new collection of poems from Taylor Mali, the author
of "What Teachers Make," the most forwarded poem in the world.

In Search of Midnight: the Mike Mcgee Handbook of Awesome (2009)
Slam's geek champion/class clown Mike McGee on his search for midnight
through hilarious prose, poetry, anecdotes, and how-to lists.

Over the Anvil We Stretch (2008)
2-time poetry slam champ Anis Mojgani's first collection: a Pushcart-Nominated
batch of backwood poetics, Southern myth, and rich imagery.

Animal Ballistics (2009)
Trading addiction and grief for empowerment and humor with her poetry,
Sarah Morgan does it best.

Rise of the Trust Fall (2010)
Award-winning feminist poet Mindy Nettifee
releases her second book of funny, daring, gorgeous, accessible poems.

No More Poems About the Moon (2008)
A pixilated, poetic and joyful view of a hyper-sexualized,
wholeheartedly confused, weird, and wild America with Michael Roberts.

Miles of Hallelujah (2010)
Slam poet/pop-culture enthusiast Rob "Ratpack Slim" Sturma
shows first collection of quirky, fantastic, romantic poetry.

Spiking the Sucker Punch (2009)
Nerd heartthrob, award-winning artist and performance poet,
Robbie Q. Telfer stabs your sensitive parts with his wit-dagger.

Racing Hummingbirds (2010)
Poet/performer Jeanann Verlee releases an award-winning book
of expertly crafted, startlingly honest, skin-kicking poems.

Live for a Living (2007)
Acclaimed performance poet Buddy Wakefield releases his second collection
about healing and charging into life face first.

WRITE BLOODY ANTHOLOGIES

The Elephant Engine High Dive Revival (2009)
Our largest tour anthology ever! Features unpublished work by
Buddy Wakefield, Derrick Brown, Anis Mojgani and Shira Erlichman!

The Good Things About America (2009)
American poets team up with illustrators to recognize the beauty and wonder in our
nation. Various authors. Edited by Kevin Staniec and Derrick Brown

Junkyard Ghost Revival (2008)
Tour anthology of poets, teaming up for a journey of the US in a small van.
Heart-charging, socially active verse.

The Last American Valentine:
Illustrated Poems To Seduce And Destroy (2008)
Acclaimed authors including Jack Hirschman, Beau Sia, Jeffrey McDaniel,
Michael McClure, Mindy Nettifee and more. 24 authors and 12 illustrators
team up for a collection of non-sappy love poetry. Edited by Derrick Brown

Learn Then Burn (2010)
Exciting classroom-ready anthology for introducing new writers
to the powerful world of poetry. Edited by Tim Stafford and Derrick Brown.

Learn Then Burn Teacher's Manual (2010)
Turn key classroom-safe guide Tim Stafford and Molly Meacham
to accompany *Learn Then Burn*: A modern poetry anthology for the classroom.

WRITEBLOODY
QUALITY AMERICAN BOOKS

WWW.WRITEBLOODY.COM

WRITEBLOODY
QUALITY AMERICAN BOOKS

Pull Your Books Up
By Their Bootstraps

Write Bloody Publishing distributes and promotes great books of fiction, poetry and art every year. We are an independent press dedicated to quality literature and book design, with an office in Long Beach, CA.

Our employees are authors and artists so we call ourselves a family. Our design team comes from all over America: modern painters, photographers and rock album designers create book covers we're proud to be judged by.

We publish and promote 8-12 tour-savvy authors per year. We are grass-roots, D.I.Y., bootstrap believers. Pull up a good book and join the family. Support independent authors, artists and presses.

Visit us online:

WRITEBLOODY.COM

CPSIA information can be obtained at www.ICGtesting.com
Printed in the USA
BVOW071549190513

321058BV00003B/9/P